1 Introduction

This paper analyzes the manner in which multinational firms facilitate technology transfer from industrialized countries (North) to countries just removed from the world's technology frontier (South), and the role played by Southern policies regarding intellectual property protection. Recognizing the empirical regularity that industries respond to intellectual property rights (IPRs) differently, the model clearly distinguishes firms based on inherent characteristics directly related to intellectual property and its protection, which explain various responses to policy on IPRs. The impact of IPRs on different firms' entry decisions alters both the level and composition of technology transfer to the South. The results suggest that stronger IPRs lead to an overall increase in technology transfer, but may change its composition from foreign direct investment (FDI) to arms-length licensing.

Intellectual property protection plays an important role in technological development and dissemination, supporting incentives for innovation and helping to determine conditions under which technology will be transferred. Technological innovations, which are generally characterized as intellectual property, are costly to develop but can be relatively cheap to imitate in many industries. Stronger IPRs in developing countries may encourage market-based transactions of technology, but hinder access to the technological frontier by domestic firms by extending the protected property of foreign innovators.[1]

The activity under analysis is prior to the actual impact of the technology transfer on host countries, especially through non-market spillovers. A substantive economic literature on the impact of foreign direct investment on the host countries provides weak evidence that FDI

---

[1] See Maskus (2000) for a detailed discussion of this point.

generates positive spillovers.[2] In the present analysis, however, the technology transfer occurs by intentional decision of the firm[3], and the actual impact of the transfer is outside the scope of this paper. It remains an open question, especially when noting that, to my knowledge, no study investigates the impact on host countries of technological spillovers related to cross-border licensing.

In the model, each firm has a monopoly on the latest quality innovation for its particular good and decides among three ways to service the Southern market—exporting, licensing, or FDI. The influence of IPRs on this decision involves the market imperfections surrounding the new innovation. The firm's knowledge of this technical innovation is the proprietary asset that gives it an ownership advantage. This knowledge is non-rival, and others can use it in direct competition if the firm cannot preserve the monopoly. Monopolistic power of the proprietary asset can only exist as long as the good is excludable, which relates directly to the strength of IPRs.

Economic theory suggests that IPRs encourage market-based cross-border technology transfers, although, as Smith (2001) points out, the theoretical impact of IPRs on the marginal substitution between FDI and licensing is ambiguous. Dunning (1981) outlines the motivation

---

[2] In particular, Haddad and Harrison (1993) find weak plant-level productivity growth negatively correlated with foreign presence in Morocco, and Aitken, Hanson and Harrison (1999) find similar results for Venezuela. Kokko (1994) finds that spillovers are less likely in "enclave" sectors with large technology gaps and high foreign shares. A review by Hanson (2001) suggests that domestic plants in industries with a large multinational presence actually realize lower rates of productivity growth.

[3] To help clarify the difference, Grossman and Helpman (1991) define technological spillovers occurring when firms acquire information created by others without paying for it in a market transaction, and the creators (or current owners) have no effective recourse under prevailing laws (such as those protecting IPRs) to prevent other firms from utilizing information so acquired. This quality highlights the partial excludability of knowledge goods, and serves as a primary theoretical benefit of FDI (Wang and Blomstrom 1992). Unintentional spillovers, or "leakages", can occur in a variety of ways across national borders. Reverse engineering, similar to imitation, describes the process of developing a competing product using the original. This method is generally employed in fields in which innovative qualities can be easily mimicked, such as certain chemicals. Leakages also occur through defection, when a former employee begins working for a competitor, through the emigration of high-skilled workers, or when a firm breaks a licensing contract to produce its own good absent of royalties.

for firms to service a foreign country with products based on proprietary technology. Firms may choose to shift production overseas in place of exports if sufficient location advantages are present. Once firms have decided to service a foreign country with proprietary technology, they will do so by foreign direct investment if the returns to internalization exceed those of licensing.

Although there are many general determinants of FDI—including market size, transportation costs, and tax incentives—the fear of losing control of the proprietary asset is the major theoretical consideration on the margin between FDI and licensing (Horstmann and Markusen 1987). IPRs affect the risk of losing control by making imitation more costly (possibly by expanding the distance in product space required for the introduction of a competitive product) or by strengthening contract rights, thereby increasing bargaining power and royalty rates for licensors (Gallini and Wright 1990, Helpman 1993, Glass 1997, Smith 2001, Markusen 2001).

Imperfect protection of intellectual property allows for knowledge to leak to competing firms, a dissipation of the proprietary asset commonly referred to as imitation. This non-market method of technology transfer provides no return to innovating firm. Imitation could be the direct copying of an existing good, or the development of a "knock-off" product. A wider scope of IPRs prevents imitation so that an imitating firm must establish a larger distance from the original good in technology space. Weaker patent laws allow for closer substitutes to compete against the original commodity.

If the Southern wage is low enough relative to the North to provide a location advantage for a firm, it will shift production to an overseas affiliate. The multinational firm then seeks a patent to protect the new technology from Southern firms. The level of IPRs in the South affects the probability that this imitation will successfully infringe on the multinational firm's ownership advantage. Firms internalize production, rather than license or export, if FDI offers a better return. Internalization advantages usually arise in the presence of information asymmetries. The Northern firm must signal the quality of its innovation to any potential licensees without revealing sufficient knowledge to a potential Southern licensee that may defect and sell a competing product (Markusen 1995).

Many authors model these information asymmetries as a signaling game about the quality of the innovation.[4] I model the contract as a self-enforcing mechanism. Due to the threat of defection, any licensing contract signed will be self-enforcing, wherein terms of the contract are such that the licensee will be better off not defecting. If a self-enforcing contract cannot be found, firms will not license.[5] The level of IPRs directly influences the conditions on which these contracts can arise.

No existing theoretical model differentiates industry characteristics that affect a firm's response to IPRs, however, despite the established notion that industries respond to IPRs differently.[6] Mansfield's (1994) survey results show that the importance of IPRs in a firm's technology transfer decision is highly correlated by industry. In particular, firms in the chemical and electrical equipment industries consistently reported that IPRs were too weak to permit licensing of their latest technology, but metals firms were relatively unaffected by IPRs. Mansfield finds that firms in the chemicals, pharmaceuticals, electrical equipment, and

---

[4] Horstmann and Markusen (1987), Gallini and Wright (1990), and Vishwasrao (1994) are all examples of models that use signaling.

[5] Ethier and Markusen (1996), Markusen (2001), and Yang and Maskus (2001) are models that use this self-enforcing contract mechanism.

[6] Markusen (2001) includes an extension with firms that have large fixed costs, so that the optimal level of IPRs may be set to induce the entry of the second firm, and Glass and Saggi (1998) model FDI in two states of nature, where the South may be one or two levels away from the technology frontier. Neither of these, however, captures the differences in the nature of the product produced that affect a firm's response to IPRs.

machinery industries place a larger emphasis on IPRs regardless of country.[7] He suggests that the industries unaffected by IPRs may require expensive or complex inputs protecting them from imitation, but that the industries greatly affected (in particular, chemicals) may be influenced by the coverage of particular laws protecting intellectual property.

This evidence supports survey results from Levin et al (1987) which demonstrate that different industries may carry dramatically different responses to the incentives offered by patents. According to the Levin survey, the dominant methods for the appropriation of new innovations in most industries include proprietary secrets and lead time. In chemicals, however, patents (i.e., IPRs) served as the primary method of appropriation. Overall, the sectors that gave the highest ratings to patents were: petroleum refining, drugs, plastics, inorganic chemicals, and organic chemicals.

Cohen et al (2000), in an update of the Levin survey, discuss the characteristics of R&D in the chemical industry that may explain this ambiguous dependence on patents. They stress a distinction between "discrete" product industries such as drugs, chemicals, and biotechnology, as opposed to "complex" industries such as electronics and scientific instruments, a classification introduced by Merges and Nelson (1990). The key difference involves the number of separately elements in an innovation subject to patenting. In the complex industries, patents are generally devices used to block a rival's innovation with complementary technologies. In discrete industries, every new innovation enjoys a unique patent, and thus patents are the dominant method of appropriation.[8]

---

[7] Smarzynska (2000) demonstrates that these four industries will tend to build wholly-owned subsidiaries in the presence of weaker protection.

[8] Anand and Khanna (2000) investigate the structure of licensing contracts within the Chemicals, Computers, and Electronics industries. They find that the high incidence of licensing contracts in these "high-tech" industries reflects the volume of technology available, but licensing is a less likely outcome for weakly patented technologies. They show that licensing increases with IPRs and propose that cross-industry variation may be a valuable

The present paper captures these cross-sectoral differences by distinguishing multinational firms by the *type* of industry they represent. I suggest industries may realize different impacts between dependence on intellectual property and intellectual property rights. Firms dependent on intellectual property are vulnerable to imitation because their profit stream would be at risk should they lose control over their proprietary asset. Firms dependent on IPRs may not necessarily have substantial intellectual property at the core of their business, but will be vulnerable because their proprietary asset can be easily replication. The model provides similar motivation across industries for shifting production to overseas affiliates due to identical rents achieved through patent-induced monopolistic control of innovations. The relative role for technology transfer varies by industry. Thus, industry characteristics of multinational firms affect the relevance of Southern policy on IPRs.

2 The benchmark model

2.1 Basics

There are two regions in the model: the North, which houses all innovating firms; and the South, which houses all imitating firms. Goods are indexed j along a continuum from (0,1), which means a fixed variety of goods exists, each of which can be improved in quality. For every good, there is a corresponding firm in the North can produce only that good. Each Northern firm realizes an exogenous innovation on the quality of the good it produces at the beginning of every time period t,. This quality improves the utility gleaned from the good by the multiplicative value q (where q>1). That is, starting at quality level 1, the next improvement yields a quality q, the next improvement a quality level q^2, and so on. For every innovation,

---

explanation for this empirical regularity.

consumers are willing to pay q times the price of the most recent level of quality.

Firms have a monopoly on the innovation, but with the innovation the knowledge of all previous quality levels is dissipated and that good is produced competitively. Thus, at the beginning of every time period, firms own the rights to the latest quality level for their particular good, but every other firm in the world can produce and sell the q_{-1} quality level of the good innovated in the previous time period t-1. As shown below, the innovating firms set prices to capture the entire market for each type of good.

2.2 Shifting production

In order to service the Southern market with the latest innovation, Northern firms produce the good domestically and then export it, or they can choose to shift production to the South and take advantage of lower factor costs.[9] Labor is the only input in the model, and for simplicity I assume no transportation costs. Appendix A.1 works through the fundamental equations of the model with a parameter for trade costs, which adds complexity to the basic model without additional theoretical insights. Transportation costs can be understood simply as part of the wedge between relative wages.

If the relative wage is attractive enough for firms to shift production, they can choose between licensing the new technology to a Southern firm, or by internalizing production within their own subsidiary. I call any firm that shifts production a multinational enterprise. When they internalize production within an affiliated subsidiary, I call the activity FDI. Firms choose between licensing and FDI depending on characteristics of the Southern market and their own industry. If FDI is chosen, the firm must pay a fixed cost **F** to cover the establishment of a new plant and faces the probability μ that imitation will lead to dissipation of the firm's proprietary

---

[9] In contrast to Hortsmann and Markusen (1987), who use a "licensee cost advantage" for both licensing and FDI to

asset.[10]

I assume there can be no imitation of exported goods, which focuses the model on the relationship between FDI and licensing.[11] The imitation risk in the model for the multinational is defection, an assumption that finds support in anecdotal examples. Smarzynska (2000) refers to case studies of multinationals in Eastern Europe and China that fear the future presence of competing goods produced by virtue of defection. Markusen (2001) cites evidence from Hobday (1995) that many managers of local companies in Latin America and East Asia are former employees of multinational firms.

These costs and risks of licensing are covered by the firm offering a self-enforcing contract to the licensee, in which remaining under contract is more attractive to the producing firm than defecting and starting a rival plant. A contract is self-enforcing if the returns to defection are lower than the returns to remaining under contract. Suppose that a defecting firm successfully produces a competing product at rate λ dependent on the level of IPRs. In order to prevent this defection, a licensor simply offers a rent-sharing contract worth at least λ. With stronger IPRs, the rate of successful imitation goes down, so an innovator can write a contract that preserves its rents. Thus, the incentive for licensing increases with IPRs.

The benefits and costs for the three modes of entry are outlined in Table 1. Exporting firms produce in their domestic plant, so they pay no fixed costs for production. With no reverse engineering, they also maintain secrecy of their technology and thus do not face any risk of dissipation of their proprietary asset. In addition, they earn the full rents from the sales of the

---

occur in equilibrium, I assume symmetry of marginal cost for all Southern production.

[10] Vishwasrao (1994) assumes firms that internalize cannot be imitated, while those that license face the possibility of imitation. I allow for the defection of a licensee, but such that it will not occur in the presence of a self-enforcing contract. Imitation of FDI allows the model to capture the influence of IPRs on the exporting-versus-FDI decision.

[11] I show in Appendix A.2 the changes in the model if reverse engineering is possible. The fundamental trade-offs remain unaltered, but the parameter space conducive to exporting shrinks.

good. These rents, however, are lower than if production were shifted, due to the higher marginal cost of production in the North.

Licensing firms benefit from the lower Southern wages, and thus earn higher rents. They only earn the royalty rate $(1-\lambda)$ from the sales of their goods, which captures the risk of defection.[12] Firms that engage in FDI earn the full rents from Southern production. The disincentives for FDI include the fixed cost F of establishing the overseas subsidiary and the risk of imitation by a Southern firm.

Table 1: The three modes of entry

Mode of Entry	Benefits	Costs
Exporting	<ul><li>Pay no fixed costs</li><li>Face no risk of dissipation</li><li>Earn full rents</li></ul>	<ul><li>Pay higher marginal cost w>1</li><li>(no transportation costs)</li></ul>
Licensing	<ul><li>Pay lower marginal cost</li><li>No fixed costs</li><li>No explicit risk of dissipation</li></ul>	<ul><li>Earn $(1-\lambda)$ of rents, which implicitly covers the risk of defection</li></ul>
FDI	<ul><li>Pay lower marginal cost</li><li>Earn full rents</li></ul>	<ul><li>Pay fixed cost F</li><li>Face risk of dissipation μ</li></ul>

The decision between licensing and FDI is independent of the relative wage since both use the same costs of production. The incentives for internalization (i.e., FDI) increase as λ increases or as F or μ decrease. As shown below, the incentive for FDI relative to licensing also increases with the rents from overseas production.

Exporting yields rents E. Overseas production as a monopoly earns rents R, but after dissipation earns duopoly rents D. Licensing firms receive $(1-\lambda)R$. multinational firms earn R

---

[12] Markusen (2001) and McDaniel (2000) both assume fixed costs for both FDI and licensing, where the fixed cost

with probability (1-μ) and D with probability μ, and pay the fixed cost F. A firm will choose to shift production if the returns to exporting are lower than either the returns to licensing or FDI. With risk neutrality, the firm will choose to shift production if the following two conditions hold:

$$(1-\mu)R + \mu D - F > E \tag{1}$$

and

$$(1-\lambda)R > E. \tag{2}$$

If both inequalities for (1) and (2) hold, the firm will choose between licensing and FDI based on the expected returns from both. The firm will choose to engage in FDI if:

$$(1-\mu)R + \mu D - F > (1-\lambda)R. \tag{3}$$

2.3 Profit Equations

Following Grossman and Helpman's (1991) quality-ladders model, both the quantity and the quality of each good consumed provides utility for the time period t. Consider, across all goods, the instantaneous logarithmic utility function and budget constraint,

$$\log u(t) = \int_0^1 \log[\sum_k q_k(j) x_{kt}(j)] dj \quad s.t. \int_0^1 p_j x_j dj = w_s L_s, \tag{4}$$

where $q_k(j)$ is the quality level k of good j consumed, and $x_{kt}(j)$ is the amount of quality level k of good j consumed at time t. The innovations improve a good relative to itself, so without loss of generality the naught quality level can be normalized $q_0(j)=1$ leaving $q_k(j)=q^k$, where k is not a superscript but an exponent.

The elasticity of substitution is constant among types of goods. Consumers thus spend a constant proportion of their income across the product line, purchasing only the quality level sold for the lowest price, per unit of quality, for each type of good j. Firms compete in price to signal the quality of their good. The goods at technology levels q_{-1} and below are produced and

---

of licensing is lower. I assume costless licensing.

sold competitively throughout the world, and since the lowest marginal cost is the Southern wage, these goods are priced w_s. For simplicity, normalize everything to this wage, so that $w_s = 1$. Profit-maximizing firms with proprietary control of an innovation thus charge $(q-\varepsilon)w_s$, capturing the entire market. As $\varepsilon \to 0$, this limit price is $qw_s = q$.

With symmetrical demand for all varieties of goods j, consumers split their income evenly along the continuum. Thus, the quantity sold depends only on the size of the Southern market L_s,

$$x_j = L_s/p_j, \tag{5}$$

which is the same for all x_j, since the price of the latest generation of goods are all q. Profits are given by the difference between price and cost times quantity,

$$\pi = (p_j - w_j)\frac{L_s}{p_j}. \tag{6}$$

The only difference between exporting profits and multinational firm profits is the marginal cost, or wage, since the price does not change. Define the relative wage $w \equiv w_n/w_s = w_n$ so that

$$E = (q*w_s - w_n)\frac{L_s}{q*w_s} = (1 - \frac{w}{q})L_s \tag{7}$$

$$R = (q*w_s - w_s)\frac{L_s}{q*w_s} = (1 - \frac{1}{q})L_s. \tag{8}$$

With this price competition, a second competitor bids the price down to cost, and duopoly profits following imitation are, then, zero. Therefore,

$$D = 0 \tag{9}$$

and

$$R - E = (w-1)\frac{L_s}{q}. \tag{10}$$

From (1), firms choose FDI over exporting if $(1-\mu)R - F > E$. Plugging in for R and E and solving for the relative wage yields

$$\frac{w}{q-1} > \frac{1}{q-1} + \mu + \frac{F}{R}. \tag{11}$$

A firm will prefer FDI to exporting if the relative wage is high with respect to the right-hand side of (11).[13] The value of the wage that determines this decision increases as F or μ increase. When the disincentives for FDI are higher, a larger wedge between Northern and Southern wages is necessary to induce overseas production.

From (2), firms choose licensing over exporting if $(1-\lambda)R > E$. Plugging in for R and E yields

$$\frac{w}{q-1} > \frac{1}{q-1} + \lambda. \tag{12}$$

Similarly, a firm prefers FDI to licensing if $(1-\mu)R - F > (1-\lambda)R$, which simplifies to

$$\lambda > \mu + \frac{F}{R}. \tag{13}$$

This is a key relationship in the model. If the disadvantage of licensing – the lost royalties – is greater than the disadvantages of FDI – the risk of imitation and the fixed cost – then firms prefer to internalize production. The effect of the fixed cost diminishes with the monopoly rents, since the actual capital loss diminishes with the size of the market (see McDaniel 2000).

Notice that if (11) holds and (12) does not, then (13) must hold. That is, if a firm prefers FDI to exporting, and exporting to licensing, then it prefers FDI to licensing. This transitivity feature holds for each relationship.

---

[13] I divide by (q-1) to simplify the expression. Since there is no loss of generality, I continue to refer to w/(q-1) as

3 Intellectual property and the mode of entry

3.1 The relative wage and IPRs

The relationships between the relative wage and various parameters of the model determine the firm's mode of entry. The rate of imitation decreases with stronger intellectual property protection, which captures the effects of IPRs with respect to the dissipation of the proprietary asset. With stronger protection, potential imitators must invest more resources to circumvent existing laws, to establish "knock-off" products farther from the original in technology space, or to account for other effects of IPRs. With stronger IPRs, the right-hand side of (11) drops, and firms require a lower wedge in marginal cost to prefer FDI to exporting. Stronger IPRs also lowers the licensor's royalty receipts, as described in Section 2.2. With stronger protection, a firm can lower its rent-sharing fee λ. The right-hand side of (12) drops, and firms are more likely to prefer licensing to exporting.

3.2 Graphical analysis

The relationship between the relative wage and IPRs derived in (11) – (13) can be exploited using graphical analysis with $w/(q-1)$ on the vertical axis and $\{\mu(\kappa), \lambda(\kappa)\}$ on the horizontal axis, where κ indicates the level of IPRs. The interesting regions in parameter space are those in which a self-enforcing contract can be written *and* a firm may still prefer FDI.

The ranges of μ and λ on Graphs 1-3 reflect the relationship between these two variables. Consider a country with weak protection, near the right of the graph, where both FDI and licensing are at a high risk of losing control of the proprietary asset. Call the point where IPRs is low enough that $\lambda=1$ and a self-enforcing contract is no longer possible the extremum λ_1. In addition, label the extremum μ_1 as the point where any firm engaging in FDI is assured of

---

the relative wage.

imitation. I assume $\lambda_1 < \mu_1$, so that for a range of low IPRs a self-enforcing contract is not possible, but a firm can still have a positive probability of preserving its asset through internalization.

At the other extreme of high IPRs, call the point λ_0 where $\lambda=0$ and a perfect contract can be written and μ_0 the point where the firm faces no risk of imitation. I assume here that $\mu_0 < \lambda_0$, so that for a range of high IPRs an innovating firm can obtain the full rents from a licensing contract but still faces the risk of imitation after FDI. The resulting range on the x-axis is $\mu_0 < \lambda_0 < \lambda_1 < \mu_1$, which means that imitation encompasses a broader range than defection. These assumptions allow for the model to illustrate economic activity beyond the regions in which self-enforcing contracts are always possible. Appendix B considers all the possible ranges of the extrema.

These points show an inherent cost advantage for licensing in the model. For perfect IPRs, a licensor receives the full rents R, but a firm engaging in FDI only earns R-F. For very lax IPRs, a licensor earns zero rents, but the internalizing firm earns negative rents –F. This reflects the advantage licensors have in that they do not have to pay for a new plant and can use existing Southern facilities. Firms will choose to internalize only if the risk of dissipation makes the cost F necessary. As (13) shows, if $\mu = \lambda$ for any level of IPRs, a firm will always prefer licensing to FDI at these points.

A firm is indifferent between FDI and exporting when (11) holds with equality, and indifferent between licensing and exporting when (12) holds with equality. Define these two lines to be the IE line and the LE line, respectively.

$$\text{IE line: } \frac{w}{q-1} = \frac{1}{q-1} + \mu + \frac{F}{R} \qquad (14)$$

LE line: $\dfrac{w}{q-1} = \dfrac{1}{q-1} + \lambda$. (15)

Graph 1 displays these lines in (w, κ) space with w/(q-1) on the vertical axis and {μ(κ), λ(κ)} on the horizontal axis.

Graph 1: The IE and LE lines

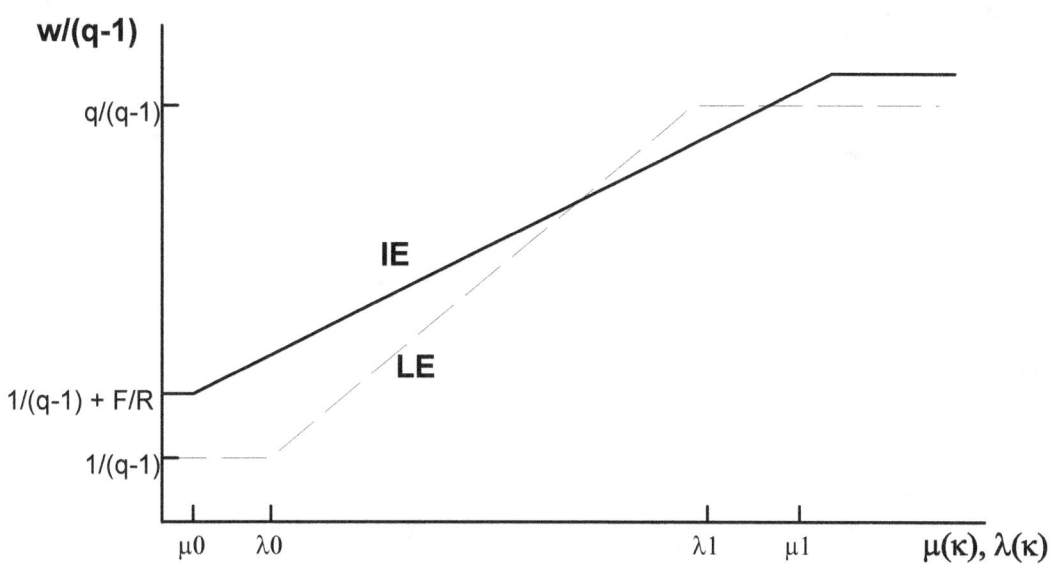

In the region above the IE line firms prefer FDI to exporting, and in the region above the LE line firms prefer licensing to exporting. The points where the IE and LE lines intersect are those points where (13) holds with equality. Call this the IL line.

IL line: $\lambda - \mu = \dfrac{F}{R}$. (16)

This line, independent of the relative wage, captures the relationship between λ and μ that makes a firm indifferent between FDI and licensing. At this point, the intellectual property regime is such that the difference between the royalty rates paid to the licensee and the risk of imitation faced by an multinational firm is exactly equal to the fixed-cost disadvantage of FDI. Following a weakening of IPRs, if the licensing rate grows faster than the imitation rate, the left-hand side will rise relative to the left-hand side, and firms will prefer FDI to licensing. The converse is true if the imitation rate grows faster.

Graph 2 fills in the IL line and divides the space into regions of preference, labeling the level of IPRs for the IL line κ*. In the shaded region the firm realizes negative rents from all modes of entry and will choose not to produce. Since both μ and λ are decreasing in κ, strong IPRs regimes are located to the left of κ*. Weak IPRs regimes are located to the right of the graph.

Graph 2: Mode of entry

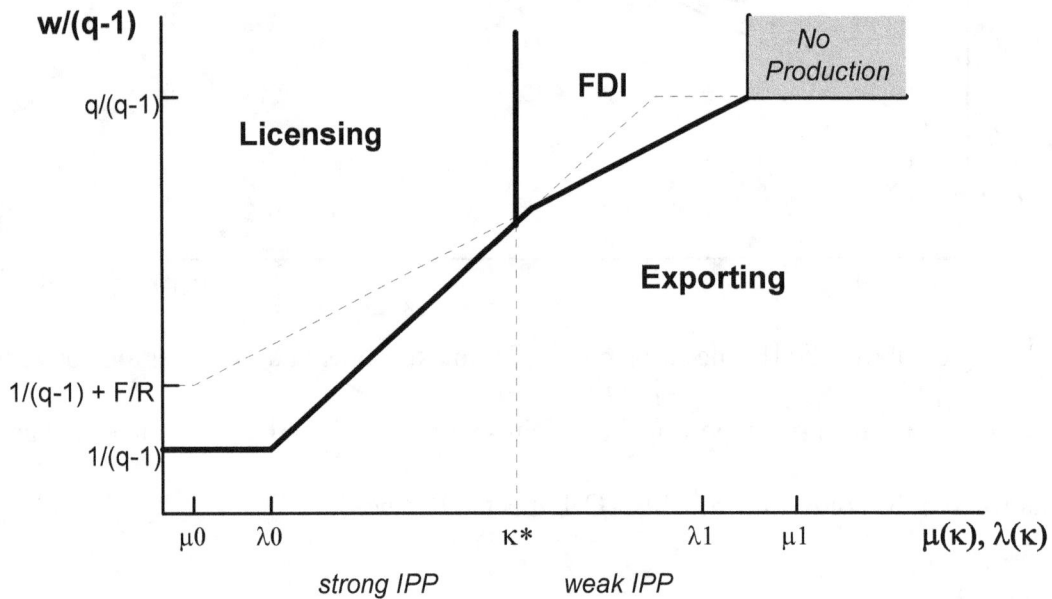

As can be seen, firms will prefer FDI to exporting when the protection of intellectual property is low, but will shift their preference to licensing as protection strengthens. The necessary wedge between relative wages also decreases as one moves to the left of the graph. This leads to the following proposition.

Proposition 1: **Assuming sufficiently high relative wages, firms will tend to internalize production if intellectual property protection is weak, and will license production if protection is strong. With stronger IPRs, firms on the margin of the exporting region will shift production abroad, and those formerly on the margin between FDI and licensing will choose licensing.**

Proof shown in Appendix C-1.

The intuition for this proposition follows the fixed-cost disadvantage for FDI discussed above. For regions to the left of κ^* in Graph 1, the relative wage necessary to induce FDI is higher than that to induce licensing. Consider point λ_0, where IPRs is strong enough that the licensor can enjoy the full rents R from its contract. A firm that engages in FDI can never enjoy such returns, since it must always pay the fixed cost F. For all values of λ and μ near this point, firms prefer licensing to FDI.

Now consider point λ_1. In this region, IPRs is so weak that a firm cannot expect to receive any return on a licensing contract. At point λ_1, the expected return is zero. Firms that engage in FDI face a high risk of imitation, but can still expect some positive value to its production since the probability of dissipation is less than one. With such weak IPRs, firms prefer to internalize production.

3.3 Industry differentiation

The model differentiates industries according to how easily a firm's innovation can be imitated by a competitor, which in turn affects their dependence on IPRs. Consider two types of firms in the model, C and M, differentiated by their response to IPRs. Every industry faces the same level of protection in the country—IPRs are not sector-specific—but may respond to this level differently. Products that embody great technological sophistication, but can be easily replicated, are sensitive to the level of protection. I call firms that produce these goods C firms. On the other hand, M firms produce goods that cannot easily be replicated and are relatively insensitive to IPRs levels. The products of M firms are by nature difficult to imitate, no matter the legal backing of intellectual property. C and M, roughly, stand for chemicals and metals, respectively.

M firms are in industries that enjoy natural barriers to imitation, and are thus relatively free from the threat of imitation no matter the level of IPRs. C firms, however, are in industries vulnerable to imitation of their latest quality innovations, and would require a higher level of IPRs to protect the rents from innovation. For any given value of κ, M firms have a lower imitation rate and must share less in a licensing contract than C firms. In Graph 2, M firms will be located in regions to the left and C firms in regions to the right. Firms that are less likely to be imitated are thus more likely to license technology, and firms at risk of imitation are more likely to internalize production.

The effect of IPRs on an industry depends, in part, on the size of potential lost rents. The mark-up q, which reflects the value added of research and development, determines the magnitude of rents. For simplicity, assume both q and w are identical across industries, so the rents are the same regardless of the sector of production, and industry differences arise solely in the fixed cost F. For sector-specific differences, I assume that F represents a firm's dependence on intellectual property relative to its dependence on IPRs. I consider this to be the *ratio* of the capital cost of production to the R&D cost of innovation, which essentially normalizes all firm-specific rents to the price mark-up q.

Industries with a high ratio of production costs to R&D costs are relatively safe from imitation. If the actual cost of production is high then the firm faces fewer potential imitators, since after dissipation a rival firm will find the high capital cost a barrier to entry. In addition, if the proprietary asset does not embody considerable technical costs, the firm faces a lower relative loss upon dissipation. The ratio of production costs to R&D costs are captured in this model by the parameter F. Since higher costs indicate natural barriers for protection, M firms face a higher fixed cost than C firms.

With industry differentiation, the IE line for M firms is higher than that for C firms. The ensuing regions for licensing and FDI are affected, as shown in Graph 3.

Graph 3: Industry differentiation

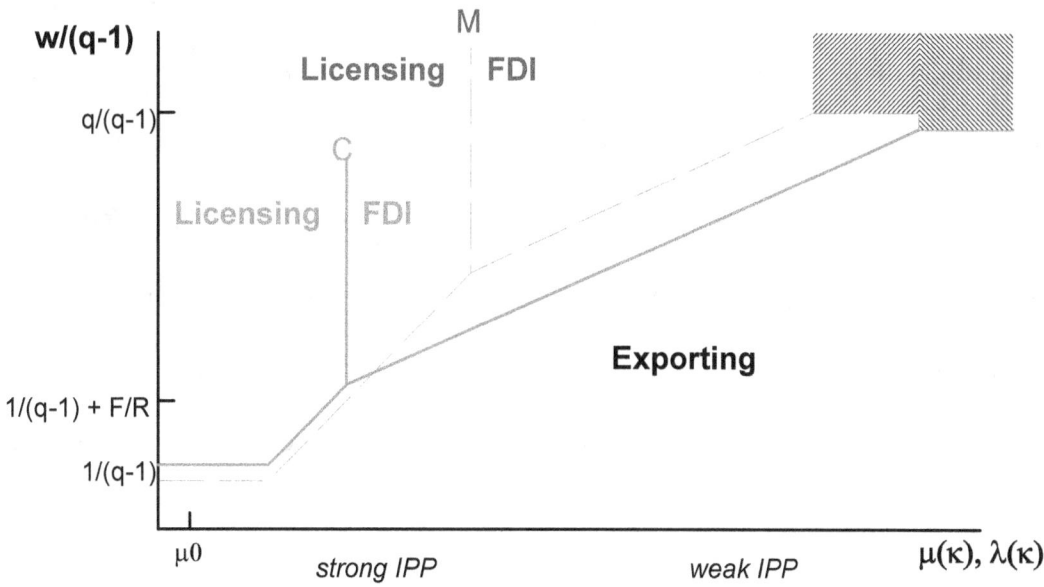

The lines of indifference for C firms are drawn in pink (filled lines), and for M firms in blue (dashed lines). As can be seen, for C firms FDI space grows at the expense of licensing space, and for M firms licensing space grows at the expense of FDI space. Since C firms are more affected by IPRs, they are concentrated near the right of the graph in the regions supporting FDI. M firms are concentrated near the left of the graph in regions supporting licensing. This analysis leads to the following proposition.

Proposition 2: Firms that produce goods that are complex or technologically sophisticated will tend to internalize production through foreign direct investment. Firms that face a lower risk of imitation, or are less technically advanced, will tend to license production to non-affiliated Southern firms.

Proof shown in Appendix C-2.

4 Concluding remarks

The response of individual firms to intellectual property protection depends on characteristics of their industries, which in turn affects the manner in which technology gets transferred from the innovative North to the developing South. This paper shows that stronger IPRs in the South lead to an overall increase in technology transfer, but may alter its composition from an internalized multinational firm to arms-length licensing. Proposition 1 shows that as IPRs strengthen, firms are more likely to shift production to the South *and* are more likely to license technology. Proposition 2 shows that firms that are technologically sophisticated will tend to internalize production.

Stronger IPRs encourage firms to prefer overseas production due to the expanded protection on their ownership advantage. Different firms choose different modes of entry due to their relative sensitivity to protection. Firms with natural barriers to imitation tend to choose licensing, and vulnerable firms choose FDI, but stronger IPRs may cause substitution between these modes. Not only is there an increase in FDI and licensing with stronger IPRs, but also a change in the composition of technology transfer.

The different effects of FDI and licensing on the host economy are outside the scope of the present paper, but there are some conclusions for policymakers that can be gleaned from the results. Since FDI includes the development of new factories, Southern countries that desire an influx of capital should set an optimal policy to encourage FDI. If firms are exporting the goods, a strengthening of IPRs will increase the tendency of that firm to shift production to a new plant in the South.

Countries with a solid technology infrastructure, however, may prefer licensing to FDI. In this case, the Southern policymaker should always seek to strengthen IPRs and encourage firms to license their technology directly to Southern firms. As contract enforcement becomes perfect, most innovating firms will license their technology, regardless of their dependence on IPRs.

References

Aitken, Brian, Gordon Hanson, and Ann Harrison. 1997. Spillovers, Foreign Investment, and Export Behavior. *Journal of International Economics* 43: 103-132.

Anand, Bharat and Tarun Khanna. 2000. The Structure of Licensing Contracts. *The Journal of Industrial Economics* 48(1): 103-135.

Cohen, Wesley M., Richard R. Nelson, and John P. Walsh. 2000. Protecting Their Intellectual Assets: Appropriability Conditions and Why U.S. Manufacturing Firms Patent (Or Not). NBER Working Paper No. 7552.

Dunning, John. 1981. *International Production and the Multinational Enterprise.* London: George Allen and Unwin.

Ethier, Wilfred and James Markusen. 1996. Multinational Firms, Technology Diffusion, and Trade. *Journal of International Economics* 41: 1-28.

Gallini, Nancy and Brian Wright. 1990. Technology Transfer Under Asymmetric Information. *RAND Journal of Economics* 21(1): 147-160.

Glass, Amy and Kamal Saggi. 1997. Multinational Firms and Technology Transfer. Ohio State University Working Paper 97-04.

Grossman, Gene and Elhanan Helpman. 1991. *Innovation and Growth in the Global Economy.* Cambridge, Massachusetts: The MIT Press.

Haddad, Mona and Ann Harrison. Are There Positive Spillovers from Foreign Direct Investment? *Journal of Development Economics* 42:51-74.

Helpman, Elhanan. 1993. Innovation, Imitation, and Intellectual Property Rights. *Econometrica* 61(6): 1247-1280.

Horstmann, Ignatius and James Markusen. 1987. Licensing versus Direct Investment: A Model of Internalization by the Multinational Enterprise. *Canadian Journal of Economics* 20: 464-481.

Levin, Richard, Alvin Klevorick, Richard Nelson, and Sidney Winter. 1987. Appropriating the Returns from Industrial Research and Development. *Brookings Papers on Economic Activity* 3: 783-820.

Mansfield, Edwin. 1994. *Intellectual Property Protection, Foreign Direct Investment, and Technology Transfer.* International Finance Corporation, Discussion Paper 19.

Mansfield, Edwin. 1995. *Intellectual Property Protection, Foreign Direct Investment, and Technology Transfer: Germany, Japan, and the United States.* International Finance

Corporation, Discussion Paper 27.

Maskus, Keith. 2000. *Intellectual Property Rights in the Global Economy*. Washington, D.C.: Institute for International Economics.

Markusen, James. 1995. The Boundaries of Multinational Enterprises and the Theory of International Trade. *Journal of Economic Perspectives* 9(2): 169-189.

Markusen, James. 2001. Contracts, Intellectual Property Rights, and Multinational Investment in Developing Countries. *Journal of International Economics* 53(1): 189-204.

McDaniel, Christine. 2000. Inventing Around and Impacts on Modes of Entry in Japan: A Cross-country Analysis of U.S. Affiliate Sales and Licensing. U.S. International Trade Commission Working Paper 99-11-A.

Merges, Robert and Richard Nelson. 1990. On the Complex Economics of Patent Scope. *Columbia Law Review.* 25(1): 1-24.

Smarzynksa, Beata. 2000. Composition of Foreign Direct Investment and Protection of Intellectual Property Rights: Evidence from Transition Economies. Mimeo, World Bank.

Smith, Pamela J. 2001. How do foreign patent rights affect U.S. exports, affiliate sales, and licenses? *Journal of International Economics* 55(2).

Vishwasrao, Sharmila. 1994. Intellectual Property Rights and the Mode of Technology Transfer. *Journal of Development Economics* 44: 381-402.

Wang, Jian-Ye, and Magnus Blomström. 1992. Foreign Investment and Technology Transfer. *European Economic Review* 36: 137-155.

Yang, Guifang and Keith Maskus. 2001a. Intellectual Property Rights, Licensing, and Innovation in an Endogenous Product Cycle Model. *Journal of International Economics* 53(1): 169-188.

Appendix A

Appendix A.1 Transportation costs and non-traded goods

For simplicity, I have assumed zero transportation costs in the main model. In this section, I show that including theses costs simply adds a nuisance parameter to the model. Reproduce the fundamental equations (1) – (3) as

$$(1-\mu)R - F > E \tag{A1}$$

$$(1-\lambda)R > E \tag{A2}$$

$$(1-\mu)R - F > (1-\lambda)R. \tag{A3}$$

Suppose exporting firms face iceberg transportation costs τ for each good sold. The marginal cost for Northern production becomes $w_n\tau$, with a relative cost difference $w_n\tau/w_s = w\tau$. Rewriting the profit equations (7) and (8)

$$E = (1 - \frac{w}{q}\tau)L_s \tag{A4}$$

$$R = (1 - \frac{1}{q})L_s. \tag{A5}$$

Thus, (10) becomes

$$R - E = (w\tau - 1)\frac{L_s}{q}. \tag{A6}$$

Plugging this into the IE line (A1) and the LE line (A2) yields

$$\frac{w}{q-1}\tau > \frac{1}{q-1} + \mu + \frac{F}{R} \tag{A7}$$

$$\frac{w}{q-1}\tau > \frac{1}{q-1} + \lambda. \tag{A8}$$

The IL line does not change. Transportation costs simply scale the relative wage upward.

Notice that some values of τ lead to the presence of non-traded goods in the model. This occurs if exporting is preferred to FDI and licensing (neither A7 nor A8 hold) but exporting yields negative rents due to the high transportation costs. If exporting yields negative rents, then

$$(1-\frac{w}{q}\tau)L_s < 0; \tag{A9}$$

thus, goods are non-traded if $\tau > q/w$.

Appendix A.2 Reverse engineering

In the main paper, I have assumed that exporting firms are free from the risk of imitation. This assumption, common in the literature, greatly simplifies the overall equations without reducing the model's explanatory power. In this section, I show the results when considering the possibility of reverse engineering.

Suppose exporting firms face the risk of imitation m. The expected rents from exporting, formerly E, are now (1-m)E. The IE line from (1) can be rewritten

$$(1-\mu)R - F > (1-m)E \tag{A10}$$

Plugging in the profit equations (7) and (8) yields

$$\frac{w}{q-1} > \frac{1}{q-1} + \frac{F}{R} + \mu - m(\frac{q-w}{q-1}). \tag{A11}$$

The IE line shifts down, making firms more likely to prefer FDI to exporting.

Similarly, the LE line from (2) can be rewritten

$$(1-\lambda)R > (1-m)E. \tag{A12}$$

Plugging in for the profit equations yields

$$\frac{w}{q-1}(1-m) > \frac{1}{q-1} + \lambda. \tag{A13}$$

The LE line shifts down, making firms more likely to prefer licensing to exporting.

As would be expected, the possibility for reverse engineering that lowers the returns to exporting decreases the regions in parameter space that firms would be likely to export. An interesting addendum to this discussion considers the possibility that reverse engineering and imitation after FDI occur at the same rate, if $\mu = m$. In this scenario, the IE line can be written

$$\frac{w}{q-1} > \frac{1}{q-1} + \frac{F}{(1+\mu)R} \tag{A14}$$

and the LE line can be written

$$\frac{w}{q-1}(1-\mu) > \frac{1}{q-1} + \lambda. \tag{A15}$$

The presence of μ as a variable in the denominator of the equations of these two lines makes Graph 3 considerably more complicated. The IE line is now increasing and convex, with the IL line decreasing and concave. The firm's decision-making process, however, does not change.

Appendix B The various ranges of κ

Section 3.2 discusses the range of μ and λ used in the paper. The assumption $\mu_0 < \lambda_0 < \lambda_1 < \mu_1$ permits the model to discuss the regions in which FDI may take place but a self-enforcing contract may not be possible. Of the potential ranges on IPRs, this assumption best reflects the actual activity of firms.

In this appendix, I consider the other possible ranges of κ that lead to different scenarios in the graphs. In general, the propositions of Section 3 are robust to these different cases. I discuss the exceptions in turn. The following is an exhaustive list of the possibilities.

Case (i): $\mu_0 < \lambda_0 < \lambda_1 < \mu_1$

Case (ii): $\lambda_0 < \mu_0 < \mu_1 < \lambda_1$

Case (iii): $\mu_0 < \lambda_0 < \mu_1 < \lambda_1$

Case (iv): $\lambda_0 < \mu_0 < \lambda_1 < \mu_1$

Case (v): $\mu_0 < \mu_1 < \lambda_0 < \lambda_1$

Case (vi): $\lambda_0 < \lambda_1 < \mu_0 < \mu_1$

The main section of the paper uses case (i). In case (ii), the range of self-enforcing contracts is larger than the range at which imitation of FDI is possible, just the opposite of case (i). As can be seen in Graph B-1, the biggest effect is a new licensing region at the right of the graph.

Graph B-1: Mode of entry in case (ii)

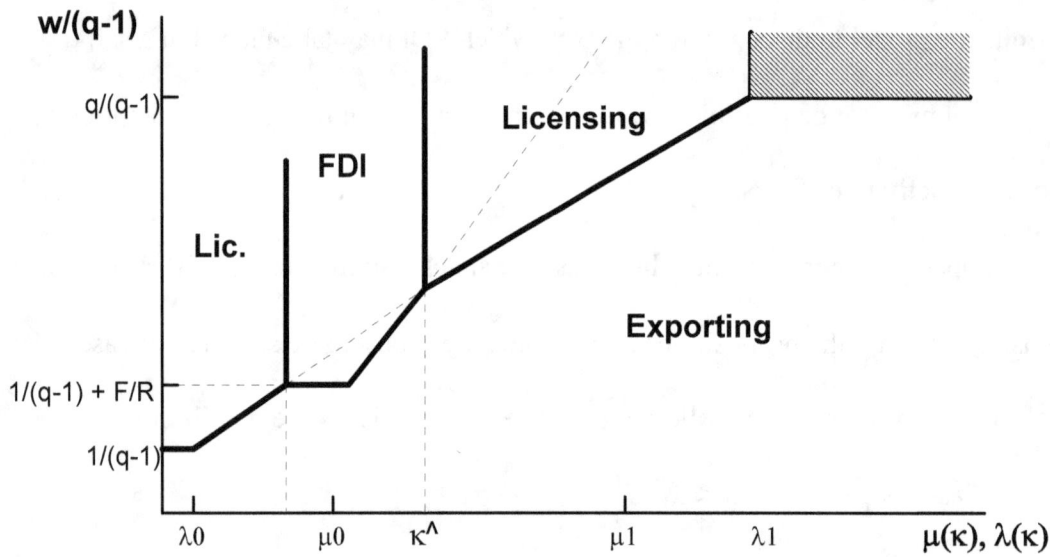

This region may tend to contradict Proposition 1, since firms in this new region will substitute FDI for licensing as IPRs strengthens. The point $\kappa^\wedge$, however, is that at which the return to FDI is exactly zero, when the probability of imitation is so high that the expected rents are just equivalent to the fixed cost. In the region to the right, the returns to FDI are negative, so a firm will prefer to write a licensing contract that at worst gives it zero rents. Although possible, this scenario is implausible, since a firm would unlikely license its innovation for a miniscule return.

In case (iii), the risk of imitation is always greater than the risk of defection, for all values of κ. A firm paying a fixed cost for FDI faces a greater risk of losing control of its asset. As shown in Graph B-2, firms will thus always prefer licensing to FDI.

Graph B-2: Mode of entry in case (iii)

In case (iv), the risk of defection is always greater than the risk of imitation, with the results depicted in Graph B-3.

Graph B-3: Mode of entry in case (iv)

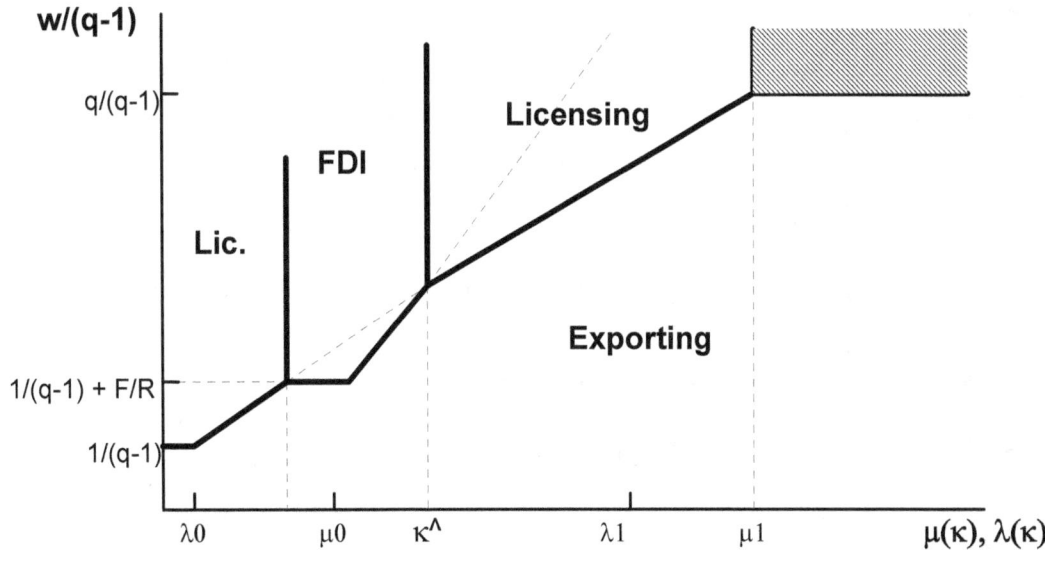

Cases (v) and (vi) are both implausible scenarios. In case (v), $\mu^1 < \lambda^0$, so that for a particular range of IPRs a firm can write a perfect contract but faces assured imitation under internalization. In case (vi), there is a range at which a firm faces no risk of imitation but cannot write a feasible contract. These cases are depicted in Graphs B-4 and B-5, respectively.

Graph B-4: Mode of entry in case (v)

Graph B-5: Mode of entry in case (vi)

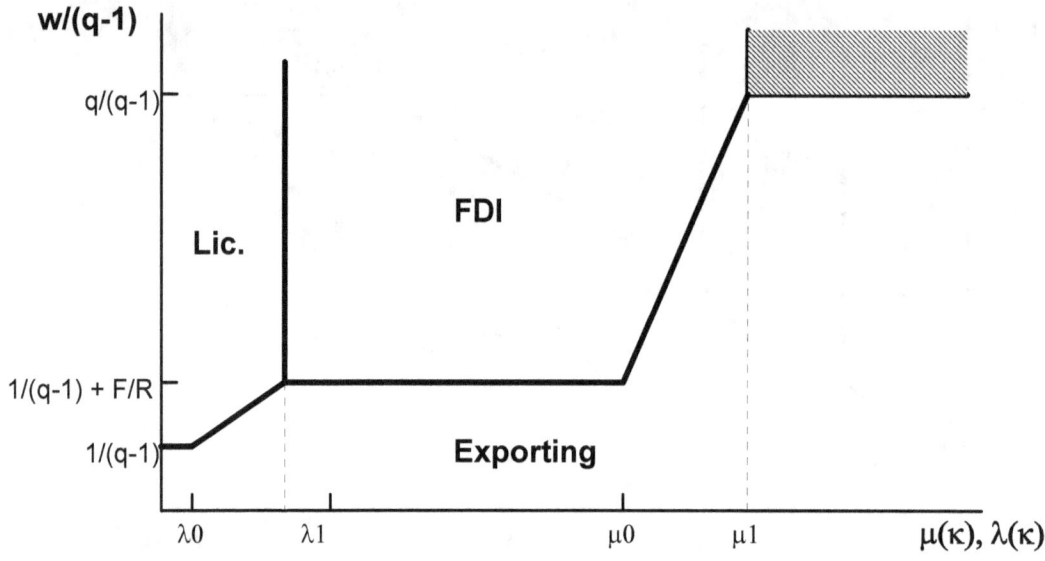

Appendix C

Appendix C.1 Functional Forms of $\mu(\kappa)$ and $\lambda(\kappa)$

The key equations of Section 3 are:

$$\frac{w}{q-1} = \frac{1}{q-1} + \mu(\kappa) + \frac{F}{R} \tag{C1}$$

$$\frac{w}{q-1} = \frac{1}{q-1} + \lambda(\kappa) \tag{C2}$$

$$\lambda(\kappa) - \mu(\kappa) = \frac{F}{R}. \tag{C3}$$

(C3) shows that firms will be indifferent between FDI and licensing if the difference in the disadvantages of licensing over FDI exactly offset the fixed cost of FDI. The major disadvantage of licensing is that it is easier to break a contract than it is to imitate at a given level of κ. The value of κ that sets (C3) equal is labeled κ^*.

The regions of IPRs are bounded by the extrema (μ_0, μ_1) and (λ_0, λ_1), which are in fact the values of κ that solve the functions $\lambda(\kappa)$ and $\mu(\kappa)$ for $(0,1)$. That is,

$$\mu(\mu_0) = 0 \quad \text{(no imitation)} \tag{C4}$$

$$\lambda(\lambda_0) = 0 \quad \text{(perfect contracts)}$$

$$\mu(\mu_1) = 1 \quad \text{(perfect imitation)}$$

$$\lambda(\lambda_1) = 1 \quad \text{(no enforceable contracts)}.$$

Since the functions $\mu(\kappa)$ and $\lambda(\kappa)$ are negative in IPRs, the extrema have the following relationship:

$$\mu_1 < \lambda_1 < \kappa^* < \lambda_0 < \mu_0. \tag{C5}$$

This appears to be the opposite relationship than on the graphs in Section 3, but notice that the x-axis represents μ and λ, while (C5) represents relationships in κ.

Consider the following functional forms for $\mu(\kappa)$ and $\lambda(\kappa)$:

$$\lambda(\kappa) = \alpha - \beta\kappa \qquad (C6)$$

$$\mu(\kappa) = \gamma - \delta\kappa. \qquad (C7)$$

Solving for the extrema gives

$$\mu_0 = \alpha/\beta, \; \mu_1 = (\alpha-1)/\beta \qquad (C8)$$

$$\lambda_0 = \gamma/\delta, \; \lambda_1 = (\gamma-1)/\delta.$$

The assumption that $\lambda(\kappa)$ has a steeper slope than $\mu(\kappa)$, which allows for the space of imitable FDI to be larger than the space of enforceable contracts, requires that $\lambda_1 - \lambda_0 < \mu_1 - \mu_0$. This means that $\beta > \delta$, and since $\lambda_0 > \mu_0$, we must also have $\alpha > \delta$. Basically, this means that $\lambda(\kappa)$ is greater than $\mu(\kappa)$ for low values of κ, but decreases at a faster rate. For low IPRs, the royalty returns $(1-\lambda)$ are lower than the expected value of FDI, so firms will tend to internalize production, but the royalty rate increases with κ until licensing dominates the fixed cost of FDI.

Graph C-1 shows the mode of entry in (w, κ) space. Notice that the graph is a reflection of Graph 2, since the x-axis is increasing in κ.

Graph C-1: Mode of entry

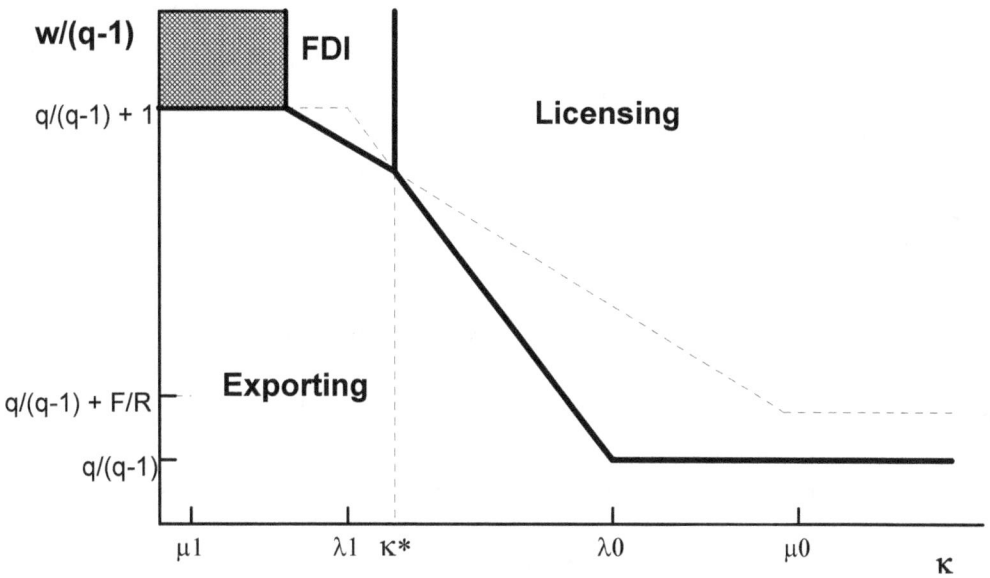

I can solve for κ^* with these functional forms. Plug in to (C3) to get

$$\alpha - \beta\kappa^* - (\gamma - \delta\kappa^*) = \frac{F}{R}, \tag{C9}$$

which solves to

$$k^* = \frac{\alpha - \gamma}{\beta - \delta} - \frac{F/R}{\beta - \delta}. \tag{C10}$$

Since $\alpha > \gamma$ and $\beta > \delta$, $\kappa^* > 0$.

This result yields the following formal representation of Proposition 1.

Proposition C-1: For given $(w/(q-1), F/R)$, firms will prefer FDI to licensing if $\lambda - \mu > F/R$. Assume the functional forms $\lambda(\kappa) = \alpha - \beta\kappa$ and $\mu(\kappa) = \gamma - \delta\kappa$, where $\beta > \delta$ to ensure the range of enforceable contracts is contained within the range of imitation of FDI. Firms are indifferent between FDI and licensing if $\kappa = \kappa^*$, where $k^* = \frac{\alpha - \gamma}{\beta - \delta} - \frac{F/R}{\beta - \delta}$. If $\kappa > \kappa^*$, firms prefer licensing to FDI. If $\kappa < \kappa^*$, firms prefer licensing to FDI.

Appendix C-2 Industry Differences

Since industry differences arise solely in the fixed cost F, I assume $F_M > F_C$. With the same functional forms as Appendix C-1, have

$$k^* = \frac{\alpha-\gamma}{\beta-\delta} - \frac{F/R}{\beta-\delta}. \tag{C11}$$

Thus $\kappa_M^* < \kappa_C^*$. This leads to the following formal representation of Proposition 2.

Proposition C-2: For a given (w, q, λ(κ), μ(κ)), firms will prefer FDI to licensing if κ<κ*.

Assume $F^M > F^C$ to represent natural barriers to imitation. From Proposition C-1,

$k^* = \frac{\alpha-\gamma}{\beta-\delta} - \frac{F/R}{\beta-\delta}$. Thus, $\kappa_C^* - \kappa_M^* = \frac{(F^M - F^C)/R}{\beta-\delta} > 0$. **There exists a range of IPRs, κ_M^* < κ < κ_C^*, such that if the relative wage is favorable to shifting production, then M firms will license and C firms will engage in FDI.**

www.ingramcontent.com/pod-product-compliance
Lightning Source LLC
Chambersburg PA
CBHW081809170526
45167CB00008B/3388